Just a moment, please…

Poems by Becky Plate

Spartan
Press

Spartan Press
Kansas City, Missouri
spartanpresskc.com

Spartan
Press

Author photo: Becky Plate
Cover image: Becky Plate
Title page image: Becky Plate

Acknowledgments:

Many thanks to the writers, musicians and artists, the countless creative humans who have allowed me to spend a lifetime hovering close by. And to Amy Isenburg for being my personal park ranger of the prairie. This place, its people and its past are a constant inspiration. Special thanks to Jason Ryberg of Spartan Press for many things, patience being near the top of the list.

Table of Contents:

For Dean and the others who have gone on ahead.

Just a moment please…

Thanks be.

Thanks be to the river,
and to the crickets and the cicadas.
To the breeze for which
the canopy trembles
and sheds whatever has served its purpose.

Thanks be to the shadow and the light.
To the sounds of solitude,
and to the taunting buzz of the hummingbird.
To hot food and cool water.
To strangers,
to friends.

Thanks be to work and to rest.
To the curl of a paperback
read in humid air.
To the taste of burnt coffee
and the smell of a two-stroke motor.

Thaw.

Black rubber muck boots
are lined with prickles of hay
that wool socks are no match for.

There is ice to break,
but so thin, it doesn't show
until it is fractured.

A moment alone
fills my nostrils with
the smell of cold, malleable mud
and my ears with the
crunch of barely frozen,
freshly-laid gravel.

Everywhere you look,
there are little pools of her sweat gathering,
congregating right out in the open
for everyone to see.

There is a hint,
a grunt under her breath,
that she is giving in,
growing weary.

The beasts are beginning to shed,
taunting her every effort.

A thump on the back
and a million dust mite angels
take flight on the warm updraft
in a sparkling shaft of defiance.

Take that, you frigid bitch.

Spring in northeast Kansas.

Spring blew into the central plains on the squall line
of a low-pressure system, with an unheeded warning
at its crest and static electricity on its heels.

The remnants of last year's wooly sedge and
switchgrass and little bluestem are a fortress of
confusion and camouflage for an ecosystem of the
intentionally unseen.

Red winged black birds perch atop nothing, shouting
their *conk-la-reeeee* and searching for a place and a
partner to bed in the reeds while a statue-still bittern
hopes to be mistaken for scenery.

Nesting pairs of teals and mallards land with a flare
on the still surfaces of shallow wetlands, twinkling
from behind a curtain of bulrushes.

The serviceberry and willow burst cordial blooms
and delicate foliage from their flesh, a contrasted
offering to the senses against the sharp backdrop of
bare honey locust and hawthorn.

The din of cricket frogs and chorus frogs lay down
the rhythm section for a melody made of the scurrying
of hidden shrews and slithering racers, the ripples of
turtles slipping into creeks and jays drawing attention
to themselves.

In the dusky twilight, clouds of almost invisible individual insects invite the aerial predation of green darners, flashing flamboyant bodies of iridescent chartreuse and electric blue.

Dutchman's breeches and trout lilies pepper the path's edges for an ephemeral blink of an eye as early bouquets of upright phlox and shoots of too soon to tell make promises of the yet to come.

Gasconade at dawn.

There is a fine layer of fog,
insistent upon traveling upstream,
against the current of the Gasconade.

Yellow is the first color of morning,
when green and brown are still black and white.
It is the corn tassels on the crowns
of the field across the way,
the stippled decoration of the
hedgerow flowers this side of the river.
It is a statement,
the very color of summer,
of sun.
And it is the edges of leaves
on the trees lining the far bank,
a reminder that summer is at an end.

Some member of the raptor family
is the first solo to rise above the
indistinguishable chorus of birds chattering
and insects vibrating at alarming frequencies.
A dog barks low and deliberate in contrast.
A woodpecker drums,
another answers,
a crow.

The sun crests the ridge at my back,
and the tops of the trees glow
in blinding reflection.
The resulting exchange of heat and moisture
has a random rhythm all its own,
like popcorn in the distance,
like the plunk of rain on fiberglass.

The trees in tornado alley.

I'll thank you to cover yourself
come springtime.
It will be most welcome
to be relieved of the sight of your bones,
cracked and splintered,
twisted and stripped of their flesh,
and splayed in unnatural forms
that catch in my throat
every
single
day.

Much like the darkness of night
offers a certain comfortable cover,
obscuring truth and terror,
surely a verdant drapery of denial
will draw the corner of my eye
less diligently than your blatantly threatening nakedness,
even in the light of day.
Never mind whatever deformity
will still be detectable of your clothed silhouette.

What good is to be gained
by your bleached and bent warnings?
By your creaking and howling of helplessness?
By your bubbling in the back of my brain
and your flashing of mangled limbs
reaching for my face,
offering fear from all four directions?

What's done is done,
and what could be has been.
So cover yourself!
I beg of you!
Or if you will not,
then have the decency
to let loose of this life,
and lay down in the earth,
the generosity to descend and decay,
that you may nurture something
new and beautiful again,
and haunt me no more
with your suggestions
of how bad it might have been,
and your omens of what might be
the next time.

I am full up on
your foreboding brokenness,
and I will have it no more.
Mend or be gone!
I cannot look at you any longer.

Sunrise declined.

The sun rises in the east
over the water,
but the clouds rise to meet it,
swollen, gluttonous, greedy,
and it cannot break free of them.

The sun whispers a story,
hums a familiar tune,
but declines the opportunity
to show what it can really do:

Cancer,
chlorophyll,
shadow,
faded grade school bulletin board,
tomorrow.

Just a moment please…

Those last few waking moments are mine.
I will keep them.

They were simple.
They were important.

Half of a ham and cheese on Wonder Bread
A banana
Sherbet
Iced tea

"It tastes good."
you said.
I hoped that was true.

In those last few waking moments
I washed your face,
brushed your teeth,
brushed your hair.

Things that had seemed comparatively unimportant
    for days.
They were simple.
They were important.

While I thought you were sleeping,
I massaged your feet,

your hands,
painted your fingernails.

"That feels good."
you said.
I had thought you were asleep.

You were determined, until the last few waking
     moments,
that one hundred and one
might be one better than one hundred.

That wasn't an option,
so I explained it again,
the things we could do.

"This is my nurse."
you said,
to everyone who came in the room.

We both needed me to be there,
reading a book,
eating the other half of your ham and cheese.

It did taste good.
That was true.

While I thought you were sleeping,
you were making up your mind
to concede defeat to your body.

"Comfort... comfort"
you said,
turning your face to mine.

They were the last few waking moments,
out of more than a hundred years
of wisdom and wandering
and wonder-filled moments.

They were simple.
They were important.
They were ours.
I will keep them.

My hometown.

Longhorns linger in the grass
on the corner, under the shade of a giant tree,
lounging there with the lamas
and talking behind the camels' backs,
spitting in the general direction
of the miniature donkeys that reside
diagonal across the intersection,
with their even more miniature babies
and the crosses borne on their spines.

In my bed, in the night
the coyotes cackle and shriek
in the way that they do,
in the way that you can only imagine
that they are in some sort of collective canine crisis.
But they are not.
That is just the way they sound.
And if you know the stories,
then you know that they cry for the stars
and not for the moon,
and given the opportunity,
I cry along with them.
How could you not?
Given the enormity and the clarity,
given the brilliant melancholy of meteorites and
    milky ways,
even in the streetlamp light of my back yard.

The air and the vapor taste different here, tastes
    sweeter
when they have been filtered through
the xylem and the phloem of the neighbor's field,
and the corn and the soy and the wheat,
each in turn, have their own distinct corner
on the palate of my breath.
Even the weeds, even the hen-bit and the yellow
    rocket
and the purple clover get their turn to flavor the
    atmosphere here.

I did not grow up in this place.
This is not the house where I was born,
not where I learned to ride a bike or had my first
    kiss.
This is not the town where I went to high school or
    confirmation,
or where I became a mother, not where I was
    broken.

I am a transplanted shrub amongst
deep-rooted family trees who's branches
seem to fork in endless intricate patterns.
But in their shade, I have spread my own roots
and healed once-splintered dissections.
I have found a home I did not know I was missing.
And it is mine, and I know it well, and it knows me.

The amber path.

The day was golden,
the sun's warmth melting the tension from my shoulders,
dripping, rolling down in little pearls to the small of
    my back.

There was a breeze,
refreshing, cool on my face, brushing my hair back,
and kissing me on the neck, just below my ear, like
    a lover might do.

The path was easy,
level, more like going home than going from it.
I slipped effortlessly into my place, as if I had never
    left it.

Secrets were spoken,
out loud and without bothering to whisper,
and a new strength, that I could not put my finger on,
    burned in my muscles.

Demons were faced,
old and new, and though not defeated, they surrendered
    to me for the day,
or perhaps I to them, and found some peace in
    that radiant, amber place.

Black Silk Fedora.

There is a beautiful, middle aged black man
standing alone on the corner,
waiting for a bus in a tuxedo
and a black silk fedora.
He reaches into the inside pocket of his jacket
and pulls out a brown leather wallet,
examines its contents briefly,
and opts to relocate it to his pants pocket.
He is tall and slender
and looks more comfortable waiting for a bus in a
    tuxedo
than I have ever been in my very skin.

His face and hands are long and weathered,
but in a good way,
like a patina.
His shirt is matte black and he is not wearing a tie.
It is cold out,
but he doesn't look bothered by it,
despite the absence of an overcoat.

He stands with one leg a bit in front of the other,
a knee slightly bent,
making the sunlight and shadow fall nicely on his
    frame,
nicely on the tuxedo.
His left hand goes into his hip pocket and rests there,

rumpling up the side of his jacket a bit.
Somehow, this casual, carefree posture improves
the effect of the formal suit,
and he is a statue.

Only the fog of his breath against the cold, dry
atmosphere
and the occasional shift of weight give him away.

The light is green. The moment is gone.

Unopened mail.

The bulbs are bright
in the tight space allowed
by the bathroom walls,
and it makes her flesh
appear more pale than usual,
every shallow violet vein
peeking through the translucent veil.

She dabs a bit more makeup beneath her eyes
and takes off her socks.
The tile is cold on bare soles.
She takes a last deep drag from a Pall Mall
and glides through the door.
He has opened the shade,
and the canary yellow walls reflect
more light than is strictly necessary.

He fidgets in the corner
as she walks across the room.
Peeling a white cotton robe
from her upright frame,
discloses pink railroad tracks.
They remind him of lips.
She shoots a look over a shoulder
and asks in a placid tone,
"Where do you wanna do this?"

A nervous giggle escapes his throat.
She shifts from one foot to the other,
a slender hand curved around the shelf of a hip,
standing between two four-poster beds,
sizing them up for firmness.
Her mind wanders to a checkbook
and a pile of unopened mail.

He asks what he is allowed.

Boxing pointlessly.

There is an anger here
so deep and thick
that it makes me quiet.

So many years of pulling at strings
and punching at buttons and ghosts.
So many years of excuses,
of comparing thickness of hide,
and I am found lacking.

Sinking into the bile
that inches up my throat,
cutting off my voice
just short of a scream,
more for my surprise
than for what you have spoken.

Hope is exchanged for reality of being.
You barge in where you don't belong.
and I swing at the air in the locker room,
for lack of your chest,
for lack of your face.

There is nothing to be done.
It will continue,
and there will still be nothing.

Sticky treasures.

There was some shade of normal before,
but I'm not sure where it was,
back where the sunlight
oozed under my toenails
and the paintbrush met her hand.

She and he have run away together,
off to the land of the living,
done with the business of dying...
at least for now.

There is still plenty to do here,
but it can all wait.
It will all still be here
long after the radios and air compressors
stop humming in our commemorative ears.

There is a slow drip of something else,
something not-unpleasant
pooling where the tar once
slicked the floor of the farm house,
with sticky treasures trapped inside,
and I tip-toe around the edges...

Mistaken.

You are mistaken, Sir.
I am no muse,
save for by the bite of my blade.
By the rendering of melancholy.

I resemble little of what you know,
and will grant no atonement
for what is lost.

I am silver sweet poison
to rest heavy on your lips
and burn between your tongue
and your teeth.

You will drink me in,
and I will spit you out.

And you will not thank me later.

Tying shoes.

It is springtime, and the rains have come.
Last night, it came down in fat, heavy drops that
    you could trust.
The sound on the roof reminded me of the hum
    of highway traffic,
Never exactly the same intensity from one moment
    to the next.
There was a hint of thunder somewhere off in the
    distance.
Not here, but you could tell it was promising
    elsewhere, and that was enough.

Today the clouds have betrayed me, hanging there,
    featureless, still.
They have relinquished their offer of tangible,
    obvious intentions,
and replaced them with a mist that whispers behind
    my back.
Something lingers here like a threat, or a memory.
As I move through my day, ticking items off my
    list,
it follows, depriving me of the shadow
I have come to rely on for evidence that I am still
    moving.

I would rather be soaked, dripping,
standing in a puddle in brand new shoes than in
this haze.

This constant mist is deceptive, insincere.
Each tiny cold drop, like a stinging little bite on the
    tops of my ears.

I have to remind myself to breathe as a familiar
    heaviness settles on my chest.
I can almost feel the pressure,
almost see the russet color of hands,
so angry and beautiful against the stark white of my
    neck.
Unfaithful, unfeeling, unwelcome, the grip blanching
    my skin paler still.
Even now, there is a taste like something metallic,
all salty and acrid, simmering on the palate.

Despite my best efforts to stay focused and keep busy,
the olive drab of the moment takes me back to Seattle,
to days that broke me.
Never all at once, well, some days more than others,
but mostly it was fine, hairline fractures, day by day
until I was hardly recognizable, to myself anyway.

Most of the breaks no one else would even notice,
only I can feel where they had once been,
the new, scarred bone more sturdy and rigid than the
    original.
There are others that are harder to hide,
like a broken finger that healed without ever being set
    properly.
You can still tie your shoes, but your hand just never
quite looks right again,
not like it should.

Of traps.

Twisting in the glue,
light glints, changing the color
of individuals who are
hard to make out
for the group they are in.

Sleep evades the trip-wires.
Squinting down hard,
the silhouette of her profile
against the glare of an airplane window
can still be summoned.

Surgical steel encrusted ships
are heavy and sinking
in the mud between toes.
And you will only ever be so clean
as that tub in which you bathe.

Going the distance.

There is a certain comfort to it,
the rhythm, the cadence, predictable, steady.
I am alone with my thoughts,
my shadow stretching out before me in the evening
    summer sun.

The only sounds are Cake, going the distance in my
    headphones,
the one, two beat of my tennis shoes
hitting the pale bisque sidewalk
and a sudden gust of wind
whipping past my head as I turn the corner.

I lose count of the times that I wipe my face
and push sunglasses back up the bridge of my nose,
One, two. One, two. One, two.
Wipe. Push.
And on, and on, and on.

I do this because it is hard,
because it hurts.
It feels good to feel this pain,
this sting, this heat, this burn.
To feel powerful.
To feel something powerful,
and drag it on and on,
as long as I can stand it,
and then, just a bit longer.

More an exercise in will than in exercise.
Absorbed in control,
forcing one ragged breath after another,
to come and go in slow, even, nearly silent waves,
rather than the labored groans they would rather be.
I inhale the hot, black pavement,
the grass, the grit the wind kicked up,
my sunscreen, my sweat.

Fix.

Warm, milky blackness swirls around my ears.
The smell of wet sage tickles
the back of my nose,
making me drunk on the fumes.
My eyes burn a little,
so I retreat into the dark,
and surrender them closed,
whether I mean to or not.

I am swallowed and swallow back,
sinking deeper into the inkwell of nothing
gulping, drinking it in
until my tongue and teeth are stained
with need and guilt
and I am angry for more.

All I wanted was an answer
but for its absence, this will do.
I have lost the will to remove
and so will set an alarm at least.
The mood is set with science or science fiction
or biology if the mood is right,
and sugar plum fairies
dance across the couch
leaving tip-toe prints on the cushions.

I rub the ache of my face
hard into the pillow
and long for my fix to come.
I am in it, surrounded, pulled up inside.
It is over too soon,
and I emerge back into what is real and present
with sand in my throat.

She is me.

She is small and brown,
her black hair in sweeps of raven
on the concrete,
as she lays in the sun
on an unseasonably warm April day.

She is stunning
and a little bit lost
between what is real
and what is for show.
She is as unstoppable
as a whisper in the winter
when the leaves have all gone,
and just as mysterious.

She is all of the talent
that I never really had.
She is quick and strong and brilliant.
She is all the coordination that I lacked,
but without the confidence that I didn't.

She is never as proud
as she should be,
and is only scared
when she shouldn't.

She was the death of me.
She and her little blue car,
abandoned and unlocked
with everything left behind,
were the death of me.
Until we found her
alive in the woods,
filthy and defiant at first
and then meek as a mouse
an hour later.

She will kill me again,
many times, before it is done.

She is me,
and all of the hopes
and horrors that entails.
And for all of my efforts,
I am powerless to stop it.

And so am destined to relive my mistakes
vicariously through her frame,
through the scratches on her face,
through the scars on her arms.

Wasted lace.

There is a plumb purple sadness
woven in between bits of wasted lace.
It is unexpectedly present,
even if its arrival was braced for.

I am spun off balance
by swirling anger at vulnerability,
reluctantly abandoned too soon
for an intoxicating cocktail
of looks and arms and laughter.

The instrument of transition
has been discarded and lost
with hesitation but without regret,
its usefulness all used up and forgotten.

Tangled color and light
and scratches on parchment,
pretty girls and pretty words
feed the soul but not the babies,
even when your currency
can be counted in seconds and hours.

An epiphany of lack of necessity
has been had and (at long last) shared.
Because the truth is
that some moments are valuable
and some pay the bills,
and they are rarely the same.

Blindsided.

There is a bone out of place
out of flesh, almost out of time.
This is not the upside of downtown,
not the inside of out there.
At least, I hope not.

Gasses and enzymes and glances
are exchanging ever-slower
for those who are circling.
A fountain takes on new meaning,
gushing, flowing, draining, evacuating.

A melting pot, a meeting place
for chemistry and competency and faith,
and whatever else gets them through,
and sometimes doesn't.

Start in the middle they say.
Start in the middle and follow the tubes outward
to their respective devices and see what they hold.
See what the dams have held back
for days or years or minutes or less.

The metal of drunken blood fills my nose
and clots in her hair,
wasting my time trying to find the source.
She bought herself some hardware
to go with the hangover tonight, didn't she?

The ridiculous are abundant,
sprouting new fruit from topiary shaped family trees
and dropping them to rot in the shade of their branches.
Little worms and bugs have built a whole eco-system
that moves along and hovers within a three-foot
   perimeter.

The truly broken are the bond, the trench,
the purpose behind the festering.
When it is all said and done,
when the adrenaline degrades down into its subsets,
and you breathe again, you remember.
And then you pick it all up, get it all ready again.

Dreams for the small are in the hands of strangers
and in the fingers that are pushing buttons
and in the alarms that are flashing, "look at me"
so often that it doesn't seem worth looking anymore.
But I do.

One vessel is closed and another opened,
each according to their need.
The invincible's strength is shattered in a heartbeat
and the lucky are patched in but a moment.
And none of them, none of them ever saw it coming,
even if they should have.

What started out as (and almost was) a
perfectly normal day...

Sunscreen alters the surface tension
and collects in sticky pea-green bubbles,
like an oil slick
to be reckoned with.

The bones are nearly spread far enough,
they have made nearly enough room
for her smile to find its place,
but not quite.

The appliance is replaced
but the shoes are not,
for lack of agreement.

Cream and confections are
wrapped around her fingers
on the basket along with mine.

A shiny red race car delivers her safely
to a meal that smells of home.

The dragging goes on
as an exhausted uniform
lurks in the doorway,
just out of reach, just out of sight.

The cargo is retrieved
as the sunlight begins to fail,
and all is right in the world.

And then freshly brushed teeth give way
to a time machine that spills like poison
from the mouths of babes.
I am caught in the net,
and pulled back to a place
I did not know that they knew,
in shock and out of breath.

KC to Estes and back again.

I.

Sun rises over Abilene.
Purple and pink in the windshield
suddenly blazes to orange.

Crops in fields in the morning air
make clouds of their own.

Ft. Riley lies empty,
and my heart breaks a bit.

Steel pinwheels keep cows company
and draw my eyes from the road,
hypnotized.

Buffalo Bill Cody looks down his nose at us,
questioning our motives.

The path is crossed by countless tumbleweeds,
too fine to catch in a picture,
or to feel as they scrape across the bumper.

II.

A young traveling woman,
a kitten and a solitary house fly
keep me company from Colby to Lyons.

She is tiny, and her voice is low.
Her hair is long and braided
and as black as the fine layer of coal dust
that rests on her tan skin and tattered clothes.

Her name is Shy,
and I wonder if that is short for something,
but I never asked.

She said that people are always trying
to give her leftover fried chicken and McDonalds
    cheeseburgers,
but she is a vegetarian.

I'm pretty sure that is not what
the creepy guy at the rest stop
wanted to give her.

Her belongings include a broken guitar
that she doesn't know how to play
and a saw that she does.

I imagine that her stuff,
in total, weighs more than she does.

The kitten's name is Dog Food.

III.

The sun is setting on the mountain.

Shadow and light fall upon it
like the features
of a forgotten lover's face.

Fine gravel and sand,
discarded needles and limbs
crunch in harmony.

Each stride accents
the color of moving water,
humming in my ear,
like soft soothing static in the distance.

The breeze is dry and warm and welcome.

The smell.

The smell.
The trees.
The dirt.

IV.

Jim Flanigan,
the park volunteer
gives an impromptu tour-guide-type speech
as the bus climbs to the trail head.

I am sure he has given it
a million times before,
and yet, you can tell
he enjoys it every time.
Every time.

He is dressed like
a park ranger,
with the Smokey the Bear hat
and the 1970's belt,
but without the gun
or bullet proof vest.

I think I could have told you
that his name was Jim Flanigan
even if he had not
been wearing a name tag.
He was just a Jim Flanigan.

We are prepared for the hike,
but not for the wind,
not for the cold,
and it beats us,
badly.

The camp is intoxicating,
and the truck is off road,
so we beat it on foot,
and that is how it should be,
or at least how we needed it to be.

V.

Boulder is ablaze.
The smoke and falling soot
drive us down the mountain side
a day early.

We wind and wind
down to the city,
chipping a windshield on the way.

We dress up
and drink and dine in bed,
but in public
and take pictures.

We are young and old
all at once.

Nashville.

Nashville is busy.
Nashville is building a city on top of its city.
Nashville has abandoned its electric scooter in the
      middle of the sidewalk.
Nashville is taking its past into consideration.
Nashville is out of parking spaces and out of green
      spaces.
Nashville is sick and healing.

Nashville is having sweet potato pancakes
and hot chicken for breakfast,
a bourbon with lunch,
and eating the hopes and aspirations
of your potential big break for dinner.
Nashville smokes too much.
Nashville is the Goddess of War
wearing a Piggly Wiggly trucker hat.

Nashville will play you anything on a vintage guitar
      for $20.
Nashville is not replacing its toppled statue
of Edward Carmack at the entrance to the Capitol,
but they aren't exactly erecting one
of Ida B. Wells in its place,
if you know what I mean.

Souls upon Soles.

Walking across Kansas,
dry straw stands in last year's fields
like so much dishwater-blonde hair
standing on end,
like a chill up her spine,
like a catch in her throat
with the clouds welling up
and holding back a bit longer
until they can take it no more.
No more.

Soles beat down,
making an impression on
the souls of us all
on the souls of the Free-Staters
the souls of the Free Thinkers
the jaywalkers
and the Jayhawkers.

Soles beat down,
one in front of the other
right, left, right, left,
looking for untouched souls
to impress upon,
to imprint upon,
to leave changed,
to leave it better than we found it,
to make our mark on hearts and minds,
to make them hear us.

Here to show them the passion in our souls,
carried through sun and rain and wind,
carried over pavement and dirt and gravel
by the sacrifice of our soles,
to climb the steps
and make the pillars tremble
at the rumble of our voices.
And tremble they should,
and tremble they shall.

Our soles are broken and blistered
but march on at the heartbeat of our drums,
at the cadence of our souls
as the foot soldiers fight their own feet
and fight the good fight,
gettin' in the game,
lookin' for the loud light,
lookin' for the sunshine,
kickin' ass and takin' names,
takin' names and speakin' 'em out loud,
until you all stand up and take notice,
until you all stand up and be counted for where you
    stand
because that is what Democracy looks like
and our vision is sharp
and our memories long.

More real things.

What if I could do things?
Do real things.
More
real
things.
Less symbolic,
more brick and mortar,
pencil and paper,
come and get it
things.

What if I could make things happen?
Make doors open,
make breath out of air,
make food out of dirt.
Make warmth,
make sunshine.

What if I could make people listen?
Listen to reason, and not to money.
Listen to the bees and not fear them.
Listen to their neighbors
without hate plugging up their ears
and sliding from their tongues.

What if I could see how to fix this?

See what lies beneath
and starve its ravenous greed.
See the beast in all his glory
and then take it from him.

What if I could go anywhere
and give them water for drinking?
Go to where the earth needs turning
or where the Earth needs moving.
And move with them
and move forward together.

What if I could be anything?
Be anywhere.
Be everywhere.
Be in and out of time.
Hit a cosmic pause button
and just think for a moment,
take it all in for a moment
and see it for what it is.

What if I could see in technicolor?
See the patterns in ultraviolet
and make it plain and simple.
Get it all written down in black and white.
What if I could see truth
like copper, in all its different shades of patina,
Fresh-shiny-tawny-new truth
and old-beaten truth,
green and hidden under layers of tarnish.

Maybe then I could do things.
More
Real
Things...

Just wait.

"Wait" is an empty promise
made when observing tangible patience.
"Wait" implies that it is not your turn,
that it has not been long enough,
that you have not given enough,
not suffered enough,
not lost enough,
not waited enough,
so just
wait.

"Wait" is strategic genocide
inflicted by the ones who are not waiting.
"Wait" is the silence of allies,
the blind eye of by-standers,
the love language of hate mongers,
the poor excuses for faith leaders
who cry that they aren't ready,
so just
wait.

"Wait" is a four-letter word
adopted by polite society for an impolite purpose.
"Wait" is code, easily decrypted,
to mean get (the fuck) out,
sit (the fuck) down,
or shut (the fuck) up,

we don't want you here,
don't know you here,
don't understand you here… yet,
so just
wait.

"Wait" is cast as a rite of passage
by the very people standing in the way.
"Wait" implies that pain is a due to be paid
to not cast you as "other,"
to not cast you as criminal,
to not cast you asunder.
Your humanity isn't earned yet,
your honor not purchased
just yet,
so just
wait.

"Wait" is violence.

Hold harmless.

"Hold harmless."
What a phrase!
"Hold harmless."
Hold who harmless?
Hold a neighborhood harmless?
Hold a district harmless?
A dictator? A legislator? A predator?
Who do we "hold harmless?"

I hold harmless the child,
eager to learn.
I hold harmless the teacher,
giving their all,
and then a bit more.
I hold harmless
the bricks crumbling,
the pages torn,
the pencils broken
and the buses rattling.

I hold harmless the pavement,
cracked and uneven.
I hold harmless the worker,
paying more than their boss.
I hold harmless
the elder forgotten,
the victim violated,

the infirm ignored
and the minority rejected
by those who would hate them
in the name of their faith.

I hold harmless
the infant
born into violence,
born into poverty.
I hold harmless
the trafficked and enslaved.
I hold harmless
the refugee fleeing horrors
that we cannot possibly comprehend.

I hold harmless
the color of your skin,
the ability of your physique,
the name of your god,
the gender of your identity,
the nation of your birth
and the love of your life.

So I ask you,
when we remember this later,
will you be held harmless?
Were you there to be counted?
Did you raise your hand?
Did you write a letter?
Did you raise your voice?
Did you tell your neighbor?
Did you make your mark?

If not, you are not held harmless.
I do not give your complacence safe passage
through this page in history.
Not picking a side makes you no less of an accomplice.
Your disenchantment does not discount your duty.
In this time,
in this moment,
your silence will be remembered as consent.

Impending doom.

We are teetering on the brink of impending doom.
And that is a bit of a problem.
You see, no one ever makes sound decisions while
    standing at the brink of impending doom.

What is even worse is when you have been perpetually
    holding your breath
at the brink of impending doom for a good long while:
your brain all deprived of oxygen,
and your body always just about to tumble over the
    edge into the abyss.
Somehow, at the last possible second,
you find just enough ballast to tumble backward,
and take a ragged gulp of air.

Rinse. Repeat. Do it again.

No.
When perpetually standing at the brink of impending
    doom,
and starved of dependable sustenance,
you are a hungry person, forever only searching for that
    next morsel,
that next scrap of food.
You are consumed by it, with no perspective left
to see around the corner of your own momentary
    salvation.

While standing at the brink of impending doom,
    you have only two choices:
You may either be determined to persevere, no
    matter what it takes,
no matter what you have to compromise.
Or you may be resigned to what will clearly be
    some horrible end,
that you are powerless to prevent;
so what does any of it matter anyhow?
Neither perspective lends itself to a level head.

Truth be told,
You don't even have to actually be on the brink o
    f impending doom to share this attitude.
One only has to believe (or be made to believe)
    that doom is firmly enroute.

It is through the mere lens of impending doom
that the blathering of a tyrant seems reasonable,
or a particular hue of humanity becomes a threat so
    real in one's mind
that it must be extinguished.
Through that lens, we cease to be human.
We cease to be humane.
We lose ourselves.
We become the mob.

Why don't you write?

"Why don't you write?" she said.
No answer.
Why don't you travel?
Learn a foreign language.
Be a foreigner.
Be a foreign correspondent.
Have a correspondence in a foreign place.
Why don't you write?

"You used to sing." she said.
I did.
In a different life.
A different place,
not far from here.
There were horses,
and growing things,
But not here.

"What's up next?" she said.
Next?
Like a box has been checked.
A box has been closed,
taped up and labeled for storage.
Six sides of cardboard accomplishments,
ready for the recesses of a dark, unused space.
Check.
Next.

"It'll be fine." she said.
Fine.
It was already "fine."
Is that the goal?
The best that is to be hoped for?
To be fine?
The best that is to be said
is that it is not bad.
Fine is ok with an extra scoop of ordinary.
I am not interested in fine.
It is uninteresting.

More please.

Excuse me...
Could I get some more please?
More of this,
more of sunny and 75 degrees.

More micro-slam,
more throw-down and more up the stairs.
More too much wine
and more not enough chairs.

More duets
and dirty old men.
More "good to meet you"
and "man, it's great to see you again!"

More lime trees
and unstable displays.
More for the ones who didn't make it
and more for the ones who've gone away.

More girl Power.
More too much hair or not enough.
More rhymes, more stories.
More talkin' dirty, more talkin' tough.

More rappers.
More 39th and Bell.

More about love and hate
and more about the lies that people tell.

More hardwood.
More fedoras and dressed all in black.
More dreadlocks and more blue jeans.
More piles of paperbacks.

More old friends.
More turns of phrase and clever hooks.
More locals and out-of-towners.
More of the guys down at Prospero's Books.

Grocery shopping.

I like to go to my favorite grocery store in the middle
of the night. I don't mean late, like eleven or midnight.
I mean the middle of the night. Two thirty, three a.m.
middle of the night. I like it because it's open even though
it's empty. I like the elbow room. At three in the morning,
I can park where ever I want and my only competition
for cart space in the isles is the college age stock boys,
most of whom I imagine are not actually in college.
At three in the morning, I own the store. I am it, except
for the occasional bleary-eyed guy wandering around
with a basket in his hand, trying to find the one thing his
wife will be pissed off that he forgot earlier.

I am not a basket shopper. I am in this for the long haul.
It's a marathon, not a sprint. I plan to spend two full
hours and at least a couple hundred bucks filling my cart
to the brim. At three a.m. I am not slowing anyone else
down while I search through the dairy products for the
stuff with the latest expiration date or stare at the jars
of olives for five minutes, trying to decide which ones I
want, which is pretty dumb, I will admit, since I always
end up buying the exact same ones. But the cracker isle,
that takes concentration. That takes commitment. There
are exponentially more variables in the cracker isle.

I like this store at three in the morning better than I would like other grocery stores at three in the morning. It's one of those bargain grocery stores, nothing fancy, nothing trendy, lots of generic store brand stuff, Best Choice, Always Save, Shasta. They have fresh tortillas and good cheese and the best meat in town, but you can't get sushi there... or a latte.

At three in the morning there is always the same middle aged Latino gentleman working. I have no idea what his actual position there is, but I always think he must be a manager or something. It's in the way that he walks, with purpose. When I am there, he always has ear plugs in and is pushing around a machine that looks like a tiny Zamboni and cleans the concrete floors.

When he is done with that, he gets out another machine that sounds like a jack hammer and is powered by a propane tank strapped to the top, and polishes the concrete until it shines. He has a system for this, I am sure. He does it the same way every time, I bet. Unfortunately, his system and my system must be similar, because we end up in the same isle a lot, and I always seem to be in his way. He just goes around me and doesn't ever look bothered. Sometimes I think it's a joke, like he must be in the same isle again on purpose, like he's chasing me, but surely not. And even though he is cleaning the floors, I still think he must be a manager. He just does it because no one else would do it right.

So I take my time, and I fill my cart. By now it is nearly five in the morning, which is still a fine time to be at the grocery store. There is still no line at the checkout, which is good, because this is where my OCD really kicks in. I empty my cart in well-practiced, meticulous fashion, making sure that each category of food goes on the belt at exactly the right time, ensuring that I can easily bag them up with the right other products, cold food segregated from dry goods, meat segregated from produce. And since I am still the only customer, the checkout man just sits back and lets me do my thing. He doesn't rush me at all.

The only real draw back to doing my grocery shopping at this hour becomes evident when the same patient man stops the belt and in a gentle voice says, "I'm sorry ma'am. You can't purchase alcohol until six a.m.."

The boys of summer.

Locks of sun-kissed hair whip wildly around,
getting caught in my sunglasses
while I drive 5 miles per hour over the limit,
windows down on a bright fall day.
Not a care in the world.

It is September,
and suddenly, for no good reason at all,
something truly terrible occurs to me:
I am not Don Henley's girl with the Wayfarers on
    anymore.
And I haven't been that girl for twenty years,
and it pisses me off.

No amount of makeup,
no gym membership,
no tummy control yoga pants,
no accessory borrowed from my teenagers
will make this moment be less pathetic.
How did I not see it coming?

I should have expected it.
I should have realized back when
I renegotiated my mortgage
or taught my kids to drive.
I should have seen then that the boys of summer had
    indeed gone.

My only comfort is knowing that
they too are driving around right now,
probably in the latest crossover SUV, full of middle
    schoolers,
with the windows down and the sunroof open,
pretending it is basically the same thing
as driving on the beach with their buddies,
in a stick-shift Jeep with the top off.

I so badly want one of them to pull up to the light
    right now,
hairline receding and waistline advancing,
so that I can look over the top of my sunglasses
and project my little crisis of middle-aged self-pity
in the general direction of their bright yellow
    Toyota Highlander.
I even take the long way home,
just to increase my odds of intercepting one.

Then I remember that the boys of summer
were almost all complete idiots.

So I push my prescription Wayfarers
back up on my face and crank up the radio,
pretending my candy-apple-red Honda Fit is a
    convertible Mustang.
I hug the curves at a daring 7 miles an hour over all
    the way home,
smiling at everyone.

And I never look back.
You should never look back.

Autobiography of Kansas.

I am Amelia Earhart,
married to Clyde Cessna, of course.

Our home is in the Flint Hills,
and my kitchen is the Oasis on the Plains.

I was educated at the Shawnee Indian Mission.
I stand tall, taller than most think, tall as the Osage,
the Children of the Middle Waters.

I strike like tigers let loose from Fort Scott, free men,
fighting to stay that way.

My voice, when I shout, is the sound of the spillway
    at Tuttle Creek dam,
and when I sing, I am a young and conflicted Judy
    Garland.

When I whisper, I am the wind that never stops
    blowing
o'er the breadbasket of America,
and the wheat sways and rolls at my command
in great long peaceful waves on and on and on.

I am a railroad of Mexican steel and black tulips.
I am Brown vs Board of Education.

I am Sternberg's dinosaurs,
and therefore, clearly more than 5,000 years old.

My beloved pets are Victor E. Tiger and Willie the
   Wildcat.
My cousins are Wheat Shockers and Jayhawkers.
These are my parents, Gus and Gussie Gorilla.
My step-brother is an Ichabod, stung by a Hornet just
   for being a terrible mascot.
What the hell is an Ichabod anyway?

I am a field of sunflowers.
I am the annual traffic jam to get there.
Totally worth it to get me in your profile picture!

My local flavor is that of a Cozy burger,
never mind the smell.

My PE teacher invented basketball,
and my president won the war.

I am gettin' the heck out of Dodge with Wyatt and Bat.
I am Sporting.
I am going fast and turning left.

I am flying if I have to go all the way to Hutch.
I am drunk on elderberry wine.

I am the Big Red One.
I am the Big Top Pen.

I am the officer's college.
I am the world's largest ball of twine!

I will write your name in chalk from the Badlands.
I will sing you to sleep with the song of the
	Meadowlark
or hum you a few bars of Home on the Range.

Sing you to sleep under the stars,
and tomorrow, we will go there together.
We will go there, no matter what the difficulty.

I am all four seasons like I really mean it,
and sometimes all in one week.

I am not a cow town.
I am cattle country.
I am buffalo country.
I am the Tallgrass Prairie.
I am the Little Apple.
I am LFK, a blue dot floating in the red sea.

I am the start of a patina on the new copper of the
	Capitol Dome,
and I am all that transpired under the copper of the
	old one.

I am here waiting, hanging on the edge of a storm
	front,
waiting with the crazy eyes and wide-open arms of
	John Brown,
waiting for the Freestaters to rise again!

I am a farmer.
I am an artist.
I am a teacher.
I am an engineer.
I am your mother.
I am the namesake of the city!

I am not just I-70 and I-35 and all that they intersect.
I am 24-40.
I am K99.

I am that spot on US-59, down in the valley between
    Richmond and Garnett,
when you drive over the Pottawatomie Creek Bridge,
where the radio loses the signal
always when your favorite song just gets to the hook.

And you, my dear friends,
you, driving through,
you, weary travelers,
you, welcome creatures,
you, fleeting inhabitants,
you are the song.

Becky Plate is an enthusiastic Kansan, unabashedly in love with the Heartland. She is best known for lurking in the back of the room with a camera, penning intriguing obituaries and hosting a blog devoted to the Sunflower State. *Just a moment please...*, Plate's first published collection of poems, invites the reader into snapshots of the landscapes, politics, joy and pain of life and death in the Midwest.

This project was made possible, in part, by generous support from the Osage Arts Community.

Osage Arts Community provides temporary time, space and support for the creation of new artistic works in a retreat format, serving creative people of all kinds — visual artists, composers, poets, fiction and nonfiction writers. Located on a 152-acre farm in an isolated rural mountainside setting in Central Missouri and bordered by ¾ of a mile of the Gasconade River, OAC provides residencies to those working alone, as well as welcoming collaborative teams, offering living space and workspace in a country environment to emerging and mid-career artists. For more information, visit us at www.osageac.org

Osage Arts Community